ROCK
CANDY

ROCK
CANDY

Jenifer Rae Vernon

West End Press

Albuquerque, New Mexico
2009

Rock Candy is the fourth publication in the West End Press
New Series, featuring full-length volumes by emerging
and recently recognized poets.

Printed in the United States of America.
First printing: July 2009

ISBN 978-0-9816693-6-6

Typography, book design and cover photograph by Bryce Milligan.

West End Press
P.O. Box 27334
Albuquerque, NM 87125

This book is dedicated to Grandma

Grace Valena Miller

February 13, 1927-May 12, 2009

One hell of a woman

Contents

VI. Blackberries

I.
THE MISERY WHIP YEARS

pumpkin

my mother used to tell me, *Don't go around like a pumpkin*
with your vines hanging all out, you'll get stepped on

she was trying to teach me
how to be more happy

i'd do my weeding chore, green beans, rhubarb, pumpkin
thump orange gourd, smooth skin heavy, green vine spaghetti

i wondered about myself as pumpkin, could i learn
to keep my vines, coiled, in a bun?

then, i wouldn't be such a *jezebel*
or a whore of babylon

lover of snakes, demonic girl
medusa kin, viny head,

of boa constrictors, sensitive,
calm feelers of heart beats

pumpkin, just be it woman,
green vine snake head,

poet, truth be told,
pumpkins are the toughest vegetable

Rock Candy Ladies

Hard-rock-candy ladies talk sparse,
but if you know their love, slim words melt
warm and gush, smooth pebble, rose petal rhymes,
battery acid stories in fast gasps like bee-bees,
words grow like pellets, because it aint all been easy, words grow like butter
soft against the rough, down ready lips in due time

My women rock a warm word secret on their laps,
peaches in winter time, fur fresh and canned
Grandma Callie named her sixth born Del Monte,
after the soaked in heavy syrup half moon hunks

Sweet women mine, rough with the outside, but so tightly kind,
pin prick fine, Del Monte died at Christmas time
from asbestos pipe dust, sawing two to fit one to get the job done,
hot water bottle breaths in and out brittle up,
useless, like two crystal glasses
left with just leather lungs, nothing-to-be-done
my mamas lose their sons

And my mamas lose their daughters too, on Rainier Avenue
and around town when the men are at logging camps, or picking apples
in Wenatchee, they lose their girls to swung handbags and hips
they lose their girls to car salesmen, lawyers, bankers, cops
they lose their girls to fire
like Aunt Geraldine making her self into a burnt offering,
after too much working, bathrobe and cigarette ember, liquor
but angels rise white winged from flame, come in breathing cool

Aunt Geraldine met one in a motel room
when her man was *beating me so bad why I just lay down on the bed*

3

I didn't have the strength in me to fight him no more see
I just gave up decided why that was gonna be it for me, but you know what?
A policeman broke down the door
and he was an angel see because he saved my life

Hard-rock-candy ladies talk sparse,
but if you know their love, slim words melt,
warm and gush, smooth pebble, rose petal rhymes
battery acid stories come in fast gasps, like bee-bees
words grow like pellets
because it aint all been easy she is so delicate
so tightly kind, suck, pin prick fine, suck, warm butter woman

Great Aunt Geraldine

She was a beautiful young woman
and folks told her so

She rose, walked deliberate to washroom
put cool shears to scalp
and cut her curls out

People said,
For chris-sake Geraldine—what'd you do that for?
She'd hiss, *Don't look at me!*

Aunt Geraldine, who could blame you?
a compliment is near lust and you knew that was dangerous

By the time you were 12, men were already hounding
catching sight, sniffing out, lapping chops

You never had a chance to throw your own lust
before they got you tangled up

Looking back on life from Nursing Home
you say, *I was a bad woman*
but I disagree

They made you pay for something you never bought
beautiful then shamed you for it, and that's a crooked lot

Just god

My god is a god of compassion and justice
a god who shames the abused, is no god of mine
a god who abandons children, is no god of mine

My god is a god of mercy
a god who murders whole families
and towns, for sins of a few
is no god of mine

My god is wise and omnipotent
a god who orders tanks and makes combat vets
for the sake of a rag flag
is no god of mine

My god loves through national lines
and languages, under fences,
in the deepest of crevices

My god is humongous,
compassionate justice
or he is no god of mine

Great Grandpa Curtis

Grandpa Curtis, they say that when you were home you drank and turned mean
that Grandma Callie had to knock you out
to keep you from beating the kids with the kindling

You were two years back in the cool belly, covered with grass
held down by the weight of a head stone, before I was a baby in Spanaway
a mile from the cemetery where your bones lay

Grandma Gracie keeps your letters home, in a See's candy box
I read ones to your wife, my Great Grandma Callie, you called her *kid-o*
and signed them, *your worthless husband* when the envelope was light

You played boxcar poker on the way to the CC Camps
wrote her how you lost, kicking yourself
and when you won, you sent money home

You fought fires in the Camps, in the Spokane summer of 1939
In the evening time, you and the others curled in warm ash near embers,
to heat black night

In one letter, you told Grandma Callie to round up the girls
and all together go beat your boy, Cody, for stealing a chicken for the family
on one hand, you knew they were starving, on the other, you knew prison was harder

Your kids picked tar off the road and chewed it like gum,
the same way Cody taught my cousins and me, when he was our Grandpa
but this time, rolled, in store-bought white sugar

Cody hopped freight trains at eight, and went to work picking apples in a wake
you'd foxed out and kicked wide, for your kin to ride—you were the first
apple picker in Washington on my mom's side

7

You arrived in Pataris by way of water, a fetus buried in skirt
while your mama worked, no one remembers her name more than *mother*
but she was strong and kind, and the two of you survived

By the time your son, Cody had children full grown, he had the fortune
to always send them out with a gold ring and a deck of cards, Grandma says,
In case they ran into trouble they'd have something more to hustle than a body's work

Hummingbird

My Grandpa used to stand and watch the red birds out window,
he never said why, but Grandma knew
She kept the feeders full of sugar juice
and never teased him for loving
something small and insignificant

My Grandpa worked misery-whips on old growth timber with Rolly Login
and brother Del Monte in dense northwest forests of 1940s
a misery-whip is a long handsaw, two men work it, one on each side
to fell a tree, took a very long time

When he was 18, he left my Grandma with her hunting knowledge and her shotgun
and my mom as a new born, in a cardboard crib,
the box said, *Kotex,* in curly cursive

He was drafted in army for World War II,
his job was to grave dig,
in Okinawa he shoveled with others, *a lot of dead people,*
smell of the bodies, bandana wrapped face, waited for grace,
Lucky Strike, cigarette peace,
never waited, for god

My Grandma's name's, *Gracie,*
hummingbird sparks red
spaghetti dinners at bottle club, his wife in crimson,
most beautiful lady a guy could imagine
They dance into twilight and make it home drunk
to four sleeping kids,
who jump in their bed minute later,
in bird-singing morning

Gracie makes the bacon hiss and percolates the coffee
he plays horse with the kids and gives rides
puts off giving lickings to those who've got it coming,
since he's been gone so long, Gracie has a list for him
That was the hardest part, he says
I didn't want to beat the kids
but we thought if we didn't,
they'd turn spoiled

Pull the sweetness from us, Red, carry on

Great Grandma Callie

Grandma Callie's peachness
softness of her hand veins
velvet skin, curvaceous
mama hen, knock-out

Grandpa Curtis when he'd done-it-again
tore his belt off, to beat the tar out
one of his eight, slowest children
exhausted, lit punk off his caulk sole
in white lightning fire, body swaying, flame wagging
declared he was going to, *burn the house down*
thud, clocked out, down for the count

By Grandma Callie's iron skillet
handle gripped tight, in her fist, forearm, face flexed
I'm not gonna let him hurt our kids any more or burn our house down
guardian angel, little woman tough guy, with big breasts and a frying pan

She named one son *Del Monte*, for sweetness in bleak times
remembering peaches, in white lightning winter
the dawn through velvet fog that always comes
Grandma Callie understood

The way Grandpa Curtis did his worst on Fridays
payday, home from the logging camp
life wrung out of him, all sinewy muscle
just enough money to head out come Monday
had to sleep outside with wool blanket in Washington rains
with the other curled up loggers, beside the evergreens and pack-mules
treated like plants and animals, valued less, than a stick of timber

11

Grandpa was always glad Grandma knocked him out
even though he'd have a shiner, and it hurt
and Grandma knew, this was the best she could do

Bullet Holes

My Aunt Samantha shot her man, my Uncle Frank, in the arm meat twice
with a .22 rifle in '63 and '89,   *woulda been an elk, woulda ran, fast er*
woulda been an elk woon' ta, done his, daugh   ters
I been knowin' his lap since, I   knew   laugh ter,
after babies and "I dos" and really after twin girls born fresh
fox eyed tiger-lily urchins like the rest

She sends grandkids home, locks doors and drinks up, vodka water pain pills
as shaking old woman on pencil high heels with thin ribbon straps
under morphine falling to clouds of cream
carpet and she's serene, in white washed memory and floating dreams
Uncle Frank climbs in through window, tucks her in
and calls Grandma

Aunt Samantha woke the next day to the walls collapsing in sheets,
her twins and her boy, her sisters and brothers, Uncle Frank and Grandma
all round her at bedside, just vultures in her mind
to force her to be clean for the twentieth time

Then the pain came like molten and made her mouth open
then the salt water ocean of pain and she wept, *You slept with our babies*
Grandma turned to Uncle Frank moved his hand to Bible with her look,
Frank, did you have sex with your girls?
he dropped his shame heavy head and said, *Yes*

There was a revolution of truth, a smelling salts moment of reckoning
in the presence of everybody at the same time knowing
then the walls turned from sheets back to gypsum
and the story settled back into the cracks of foundation

Around town, Frank is still loved by some gold teeth grins over 7&7s
but in the big family, he is no more the barrel-chested sweet easy weeper

13

nor Samantha, just the out-of-hand user whose husband still loves her
even after two bullets, because we know
Frank never left cause he deserved what he got

Sometimes justice is wrought
in this world, and sometimes it's not
we move from what we come from
and we sight our best shots

II.
COUNTRY KIDS

Country Kids

In fog of Washington mornings, we waited under Doug firs for school bus
standing at mailboxes, big enough to fit Sears catalogs and small kids

I know this because I thought it through, after big brother said he wanted to wrap me up
and send me to *the Needy for Christmas*

Mom said, *That's the last thing the Needy need, is another mouth to feed*
lucky for me

Once, when we forgot our lunch,
Mom stepped to front porch in bathrobe and yelled

Hey, you bunch of boobs, you forgot your lunch!
We gave each other looks like, *Has-she-gone-nuts, now what?*

Still, we hustled up and when we got to porch we asked, *Why'd you call us 'boobs,' Mom?*
and she said, *Oh, you silly kids, a 'boob' is a 'clown'! now, run so you don't miss the bus*

That's where boob-tube comes from, a television is a clown box
we didn't have one, for most of my growing up years anyway

Later, my dad climbed the highest tree and roped antenna to tip top
when storms came, it crashed and we lost our three channels of reception

Until he had time to go wire it back again
the water would freeze in the pipes from the spring

And the boys would dig up lines, find breaks,
warm them, try to make water flow fine

Garden hose was a clunk of useless green
the air smelled sparkling, I'd pray for snow, liked candles and no electricity

Didn't mind two weeks of no running water in winter
liked mom's hot cereal on wood-stove,

Logs crackling, flannel night-gowns, home
didn't like school, kindergarten, the fact that we had to go

Whether it was right or wrong, unlike church and everything else we were learning
which had to do with reckoning, conscious thinking
In church I learned, *last shall be first in kingdom of heaven*
my father was proud, when I hung back from siblings and cousins, took what was left

In this land of plenty, our church taught justice, to stand for what's right
at nine, I dropped out of the Pledge of Allegiance

From where we sat in square cell chairs
bell rang at seven forty five then teacher said, *all rise*

I remained seated, because I had been taught, that it was my right and duty
to reckon myself with God

And this was not *one nation under god*
and there was no *liberty and justice for all*

I had been taught that, I was in public school, which was paid for by taxes
so that everyone could go to school and learn

School was for us kids, teachers were supposed to help us, not mess us up
I had been taught that, I had to go to school because it was the law

If I ran away and got caught, I would go to *juvie* and then be sent back,
until I turned, eight   teen   years   old
And, I couldn't get a job until I turned sixteen, to make a little money
so I could get myself out of this thing,

Big mailboxes, Armageddon, school
and the United States Government

17

motorcycle accident

my neck tore by barbed wire when i was eight
motor-cicle promenade, tough skins braids afraid

hop scotch heart, hold on tight rubber grips squish, roll back
shoulders neck flesh full throttle open, all the neighbor kids watching

action, pump house, cows, gravensteins,
huckleberry red, ice-capades

my sister smacked gravel slapped hands prayed
angels opened lawn-chairs to stretch their legs

sister's voice curling, bark peeling, outer space reeling us, mud happy bottom fish
in lily pad shade, hooked, rushed, bright light judgment day

angels chew egg salad, wonder bread, pass pink lemonade
'it will be an easy day'

rascals, in poker face
i gave my heart away, was not a fair trade

they knew it'd be a gravy day, born with built-in providence
but i could only see as far as the barbed wire fence

my big brother liked to tell it, with hands on both hips
if it would have hit different, he would have reached in and pinched it

tied a knot in the jugular, and saved my life
but no point pricked the main line, track switched, and i lived, just fine

and the angels knew the whole story
before i got the rhyme

dog fight

we, small kids circling
in flannels and tough-skins

gray rocks pelting, dog bodies and dirt
dust cloud, fight, spun halo in white light

kicking, fur and blood and flesh
out of butch and chopper's grip

our little fist heart, thumps one
like a rabbit on a bass drum

Rainier Stars

Joe Hunt,
he was the boy on the blanket
when we were twelve
and my best friend, Sandra and I
made out with him from either side,
shirts pulled to trainer bras
french-kissing, strange tongue

We drank two cans of Rainier
and went to outer space
I want to stay like this forever!
running, laughing, collapsing
on wet front lawn
dew coming on

Later, Ryan Nathaniel already 5'8"
standing over us, pulled back covers
long face, jaw dangling, *Oh my God!*
our bare stomachs
We pulled our shirts down
and straightened up
somebody took us home
to Sara's house,
where it was four of us,
me, Sandra, Wendy, Sara
musk, *Love's Baby Soft*
in one bed against wall

Wendy and Sara were one year older
eighth grade elders
experienced in sex.

The next morning
I had my first hangover
and felt like suicide
Wendy said, *Relax,*
all you did was kiss
you'll learn, it's fun,
we're women now

Looking out from barn,
where we were talking that morning
the *Roy Rodeo* sign was caustic
the sun hurt my eyes
I cried, for everything
then strategized

I said, *Sandra, no matter what,*
we have to stick together at school
she looked at me solid, grave
and the next year sure enough
that was the test they put to us,
while the boys tried to ridicule
we walked tall, passed long notes
between classes, of courage and love
laughed at them, when they called us
bisexual, said, *wouldn't you like to know!*
and, *you're just jealous*

Before that, the day after party
when I got back to my folks' house
my sister sensed it, said
What happened to you?
I thought she could see
Rainier'd been in me
My shirt'd been lifted
My mouth was different, *tongued*
I didn't know, next-day-trick, alcohol does

She told Mom before I said anything
then they both came into bedroom
to get the whole thing out of me
I flat-backed-to-wall, bawled, *I kissed a boy!*
and *I drank two beers!*
I got two weeks of restriction
for my own damn good,
and my name added to the Prayer Chain

But I never told them about you, Sandra
our fierce friendship mustered through it all
our dreams of escape,
we had to keep

Sixth Grade

I.

Leander, me and you were together in school
from the start to the end, in Yelm, Washington

I got used to your shuffle, sideways grin, heavy head,
four feet ten in sixth grade, I was bigger, five foot four,

Greasy face, *Mercy Champion*, early puberty in my genes,
gave me reign, but then, I never did play you

That year
I lost Happy, too

Teacher told me, *You're prettier when you smile*
I frowned, that's the last thing I needed to help my life

I wonder what advice,
he gave you

We didn't need to grin wider,
we needed power

Shame cloaked, we never spoke about the poison in our throats,
couldn't, that's the way it works

It was not our fault, totally
we were kids

I was white, you were Nisqually, life was harder for you
I don't know the whole story

We were both, coming up country, stuck in school
and families, on the Reservation and in the hills

Set of possibilities, military, penitentiary, beauty school,
logging, babies, fighting fires

You were crackling, but no one heard
you put trigger to temple, and pulled

You killed yourself,
before we got to seventh grade.

II.

That year I sat in field with butcher knife and contemplated
how to muster courage to open forearms,

I knew I had to do it long-ways, but I was too chicken-shit,
and I never thought, to take a shotgun from the truck

I'd come in house and slip knife back in kitchen drawer
no one ever noticed, you must have gathered bullets,

Watched the ways the grown-ups used the guns,
you hunted, too, you learned some

Enough to do that trick, and permanently leave,
you know, there has never been *anyone,*

Exactly like you, Leander Squally
you have a beautiful name, like Nisqually,

The river and the people you come from
soft son, little one, too young un-done

III.
ELEGY FOR CHASTITY

Elegy for Chastity

I.

Headlines Hit Reader in Stomach/ Don't Say Why
Childhood Friend/ Murdered by Ex/ Unrecognized Death
Gunshot Wound to Abdomen
Breaking News Man Comes Home with Loaded Gun/ Woman Run
Read All About It
never got news/ worth something
and after she was dead/
broken news/
still/ come/ late

BBC never heard of Nisqually River, or the towns that bloom beside it
People magazine had no comment, she was not rich
or educated and for this, the journals gave her living nothing
not even one small "i," no letters for unlettered minds

Seattle Times spent no word space, she was not big city
ordinary woman killed sixty miles southeast, a small town death
and life all, extra ordinary
but not worth one, full page, recyclable news story

Tacoma News crime section prints one paragraph, main point?
Where ex-boyfriend drives, no mention of her body inside,
between Pierce County and Thurston,
whose jurisdiction? whose territory?

Newspaper scenery for attorneys, cops,
tourists fondle chalk, print pages, at kitchen table
tooling Sunday morning

II.

Barton boy stokes fire
with friends on Nisqually river,
Friend notes, *Logs are wet, could use some newspaper*

Great Grandma comes in struck match,
smell of sulfur, her voice heard clearly,
learning the children,   *Burn it.*

Car found by dirt mound, Reservation locked gate
Nisqually trailhead, apparently tried to escape
detectives camera snap, white station wagon, bullet pocked moon craters

4:30 AM ex-boyfriend shoots her by river then pulls her bleeding
to blue '82 Mustang, heads east, west, east, spun like sick fly
stops at gas station on South Tacoma Way,
she might have been unconscious, might have not

Police apprehend, disoriented 27 year old male,
history of domestic violence assault charges, booked in Pierce County jail

They send Chastity to Madigan Army Hospital,
she dies, gurney dead,
at 8:44 Sunday morning

Was no safe home, was no bed to snug up and last breath in
was no friend, was no family
was no *lullaby*
Run get me the moon   shine   I am always here

Frogs rhyme, ribbit swamp, front back swing pat
voice box, purrs,
Mama's gonna buy you   a mocking bird

III.

I met Chastity in 1977 at McKenna Elementary

Extraordinary sunflower kid string bean freckle-head
she had the gift of funniness, she made us laugh in chalk-dust boredom
she was a blast, my firecracker friend,
busted flat life up like silver jacks
on night-sky playground tar,
drag racer sparking stars

Chas and me eat Sloppy Joes and salty green beans
then hit playground
We swing from iron rings, hot hands zing, drop to rocks
hands on hips I ask, What's 'Chastity' mean?
Holy like a nun, she laughs
and we thunder run, with other girls like cattle
chasing scared, cutest boy in school

I remember satin jackets, hers is orange, fat teeth zip-up, mine's red
we hang them on monkey bars, wrestle, race, dare
jump from Big Toy, crash, bruised and swollen
honor badges—each stitch, crooked scar, stoned concussion

We slap out dirt, trade coats after recess
she King Tuts back to class, freckle head
satin red sucks air, flaps chicken bone kid
I'm more husky than Chastity
Grown-ups say, *Yep, Miller body, built like her mother's side*
Chastity must run from a creek of stick kin

We pass notes, wieners and butts, cuss words like bastard and fuck
my arms breath tight, in her orange coat,
no trouble, sit-still-wooden-desk

Halloween, Chastity comes cool like Dolly Parton
she has a tee-shirt too, says, *If you don't like my peaches, don't shake my tree*

My papa put a fist through trick or treat,
Beelzebub includes, tube sock boobs
Grandma says, *Beelzebub?*
Big boob you— cast ME out? in MY house?
Hush your mouth

Ham hock Chas, teeth gap grin tall eyes hop
snaps us funny side of judgment, saves our lives
from Armageddon lickins
with Nisqually river baptism, dunk rush splash
get-the-giggles fast, miracles
but they don't come, every time
Hush now baby, don't you cry

Goal one, skidaddle Yelm principal's arm size paddle
goal two, if he's not laughing, combat-vet-flashing
grab toes fast, grip eyes to girl, laugh silent, and, do, not, feel, it
never knew goal three'd be to jump a bullet,   did,   not,   make,   it
hit belly   womb   mama of five year old son

Yelm woman slain by ex-boyfriend, 28, died Sunday,
from gunshot, wound to abdomen, July twenty seven, 1998

I didn't see it coming, gag suck, hard air, stomach punch, piece of kindling, kneeling
Wash us in your holy, holy waters sweet Jesus, sweet Rose of Sharon
arms up stretch to funnel joy, heart of laughter,
can't make it here,
with no laughter

IV.

Now there's an orphan, last name of Barton, growing up in Yelm Washington
camouflage paint face, plays army,
evergreens drape, plenty escapes

Fans fire with friends on Nisqually
tokes, brown dirt rain air, bough crackling smoke, first green bud
toilet-paper-roll bong, pin prick tin foil, scotch tape

I can't get high yet, they tell me keep tryin till I learn it,
flusstrading, maybe I'm allergic
shoot tin cans with bee-bees for pings,
friends for laughs, do fun hard fast

V.

Chastity, your mama gave you a hard name,
is the trick in the word that riddles the rhyme?
chaste, in this kind of place?
grace misplaced, chastised
glory bursts forth liquid bleach

Set with a man who believed in impossible honor
provide for your woman and children, *nice place,*
cabin, doublewide, duplex, no matter,
clean, comfortable, some kind of order,
steak in the freezer, new shoes every winter

Provide for your woman, so she can make a good home
have supper ready, warm on the stove, raise up children right
Provide for your woman
so she doesn't get herself and the whole family
dirty making money in a shit dirty job

Who told you this story, so you got it so wrong? Who made it so hard?
One skinny woman?
You got her,   now it's spilled milk
your best brightest thing   could live on her laughter
weeping you miss her   rolling like river

Fallen timber,
match-stick-man boxed
in 8x4 diameter of excellent order
florescent floods, high gloss, easy scrub,
white paint, chaste right
in prison light,
right?

Chastity, me and you both dropped out at 16
I worked construction, cocktailed, left, you stayed
stripping at Foxes in Spanaway

Tripped up got stuck couldn't bust out
no doubt you tried, many times
no doubt dude couldn't tell a joke when he heard one
no doubt when he beat you, you beat him some too

Looking back bet it was better when he was in prison in Shelton
he never went off on you or your kid cause he couldn't
you were free to just love him

In cordoned visits
bring a pack of sealed Lucky straights (opened cigarettes are contraband)
change for the pop machine
Light first cigarettes by the built-in button press lighter in the wall
after that steady jump start smokes, cherry to cherry, sip Mountain Dews
sitting on his lap in the visiting room
man   could talk

He'd apologize for what was to come, a pussy centered conversation
he wanted to shrink you thumb-size, pop you in his mouth
like a Jolly Rancher   green   eat everything
he'd been dreaming about   spit shining those thighs
fingers crawling in your jeans, rock suck lips mouth pop smoke rings

Inhaling, he'd burrow his face in your neck, dip between ear and shoulder
bite sniff, wanted all of it, your woman scent, hoped if he dragged hard enough
your blue print would fold into him permanent

He got out in summertime, you picked him up, stopped for cheesecake
at the Burns Brothers truck stop, plain with no cherries on top
he chewed slow, with his eyes closed

When he finished you drank coffee in the booth,
sat across so he could stare at you, memorize the lines of your face
each freckle, which place

In Yelm by night, parked at the river bank
they made love in full-moon-light sticking to the vinyl car seat
It'd been eight years of yearning

She braced his hips then pulled belt
until silver teeth gave
soft leather slap, buckle collapse
five Levi caps

His ass to dash, back pressed to windshield glass
she kissed his thighs with her nipples and lick suck swallow nibbled
his, different dick, he tattooed and pierced it
She gets to know it
all over again, to love him
out of a photograph and back in his skin

They roll out, slap car hood like wrestling mat
he buries his head in her lap
her legs wrap   rag doll   collapse

She flops on top and eases him in
he lip talks her eyelids, childhood names only he knows to say

They turn again and he drops to wet grass
braces his legs against fender
raises her thighs to Big Dipper

She scoots and they swim into each other
in libations of sweat dew twilight

Cumming like freight-train
the frogs were symphonic
they kept their shoes and shirts on by the armpits

The next day she had faith
start over, clean slate
things will be better this time

33

That weekend they had barbecued ribs, potato salad, whisky cokes
sat around with family and friends in Doc Martin's and titanium jewelry
on eyebrows, cocks, cackled, talked
how it all started, setup caught

Running meth-amphet-amine,
stop,   *State took eight years of my life, now what have I got?*
They were quiet til somebody backslapped him
and said, *You're out now, friend*

But the women knew
that story wasn't through

They called him by his childhood name
first and middle, all the extras, Christmas supper style
no more penitentiary number name games
backs slapped   hands crunched   cheeks cradled

After awhile, Chastity and him got back in swing
she's the one who knows him most
he cries like a toddler   won't let her hold him
if she sleeping rolls into him   fist panic
no more flashlight checks
but he still bandana wraps eyes

He can't trust her anymore
he *told* her to get with whoever she wanted when he was inside
he *told* her everybody knows it's not natural to leave a woman unsatisfied

But this is just what he said, what else could he say?
in secret he hoped, fat hope blasted out of scope
that she would choose to put herself in prison, too
lock-down her body and mind, sit home and pine

For him, he knew this was selfish
so he kept it private in 98.6 degree climate,
kneading, covering up, punching down, fret

34

but like yeast bread it grew
roping sinews, yellow ragwort,
bitter weed
he could not pull it out of himself alone

He got a job doing dirt work, ditch maker
shoveling eight hours a day worth of mud
rubber boots suction, shin deep, trudge
come home head to toe dirt barely walking
changed professions

Called friends to joint venture pharmacologist
took Comet to bathtub concocting
woke up for three days gacking   teeth brittle clip plink tweaking

You were his angel, you were the devil   come to your work
like a panther, pace,   watch   you put your ass in dude's face trade
highly skilled bread-winner   better paid
bouncer'd turn him out   but he'd be home when you got there
he was always home when you got there

Once he cornered you in bathroom by your work tools
Maybelline greens, foundation, grape lipstick, Aquanet
but cover-up lies
it can not hide welts, things he's done to you

Last time boss sent you home, *Sweetheart, you know you can't
come to work looking like that,*
you lost three hundred Friday night dollars because he took it all out on you
Your kid's toes are poking out his tennishoes, electricity's past due
you grabbed ceramic cap on toilet back,   clocked him   it shattered
had a crack anyway   headwound, bled like stuck pig

Truth is, he usually won, being twice as big as you *asshole*, and he packed a gun
truth is, he loved you,
the way that broken men do

35

But you were broken, too and you're dead
and he's free alive, walking the streets of Tacoma
he did more time for running drugs than for killing you

She should have killed him first
and the State should have paid
for coffin and grave

Post-traumatic stress dis-order aid
a room with a deadbolt
for one night of sweet sleep
counseling for her and her boy
a massage, a cruise, some martinis
a life supply of Calgon
a month at Betty Ford

We should have helped ease the load
provide basic needs
for canned peas, milk, hamburger
rent check, power, water
toothpaste, soap
laundry quarters
a modicum of order

So she could use that good head on her shoulders
to get him out of her ears, nose, holes
she could not pull him out of herself alone
she needed an exorcist
she needed time for mental order, she needed rest

His words rattle ramp inside her skull cave detonate
in her opened palms
before she can make a fist she's scared shitless
she raises them, begs help from Jesus,
but he's got to teach her something
she holds them out in front of chest

she struggles to out stretch
but he's stuck like a tick tock
beat starts stops, sets aftershocks
shrapnel wedges black bits in flesh, works out over years

Time's more than a glass covered plate screwed to wall
black pointer spun white face talk,
when did this start?

She met him at Walt's tavern in Mckenna, near Nisqually river bridge
belted water rushes louder, ZZ Top inside on juke box
she eyed him, smiled, he was fine, they shot shit some then
went to smoke in his El Camino he said, *so, you're asking me to rape you?*
he took the flirt look wrong way pinned her to bucket seat
mother fucking freak

She came, then flew up in the headliner
so he would never hold her, when she was vulnerable and weak
afterwards he kissed her and took her hand
they walked back into Walt's and ordered the regular, all they serve there,
40 ouncers of Rainier

Back at the house she took a shower, stood in front of mirror, brushed out hair
reasoned,   *Well, i'm not bleeding*
figured if she couldn't handle him she'd pull Houdini magic
escape, keep spirit safe
she learned this trick when she was trapped and little
before she ever tried to exit rape

We are all free to spiritually escape, transmigrate
to stay alive, but something horrible happened
when she was out in outer space
her spirit got clipped
umbilicus ruptured
and she couldn't coax it back

She went through life dislocated, out of joint
walking tall in heels with a half full balloon—scared spirit bobbing,
skiddish off her hip

At strip club
folks usually did not notice this dislocation
physiologically it's like her liver, that 4 pound organ, was jiggling out her g-string
but we're oblivious because we believe
only stuff that's real's physical and all pain must be seen

You have to have vision to see history and spirit in present
state of heart, cracked apart
sometimes men at club really saw her
but they didn't have words to say it, it made them uncomfortable to see
what their side of humanity had done
they got lap dances and came, but their nights were less fun

Sticks and stones may break my bones but words can never hurt me
but no stones or sticks do the rape whip trick, where's this pain fit?

Turns out sticks and stones pain is little child's game
and words and fear and shame can *always* hurt you
more than blood and scars and broken bones

Evergreen sentinels croak shift
branches stretch on wind's tug
peaceful forest thugs, bear witness
to words I write into you

Pulped and pressed, pages of your story flutter
catch flame in campfire on bank of Nisqually river
He stokes coals, wonders, as you float,
dishwater blonde ghost, in bough crackling smoke
rock-a-bye, in soft gray sky
                    Your boy's still alive

38

VI.

Extraordinary sunflower kid string bean freckle-head
you had the gift of funniness,
you made us laugh in chalk-dust boredom
you were a blast, my firecracker friend,
busted flat life up like silver jacks
on night-sky playground tar,
drag racer sparking stars
you were necessary

IV.
MY COUNTRY TIS OF THEE

Ketchican Wrestling

You look like you wrestled 140
5'5, medium broad, crew-cut, redhead

My uncles wrestled, and my brothers, too
I'm standing in the airport line, watching you

You wear your tee-shirt proud, Ketchican wrestler
white cursive on dark red

Bet you spit to make weight,
ran stairs in snow pants

Cocked head, no jacket, you earned it
still, got both hands in your pockets,

Eighteen, going home for Christmas
duffle bag hanging from shoulder

Camouflage print
military's got you in their grip

Little one. My Jesus wish?
halt the combat

That makes ours Vets
and Satan's rich

fatherland

i want out of the ideology of pop,
spinning on the world trade center like a top
this is not my world order
this is not worth killing over

my dad built a house of stiff thought,
the doors and windows were all locked, there was no air
or back-talk, zip-locked he chopped, tv cable,
radio, 8 track, all store bought products

satan came to him and he changed,
armaggeddon gets closer, when gas prices rocket
but here i am, still alive,
with my spirit in its socket

jimmy swaggart cold bible lies, *jesus christ says*
they should die, prepare for the second coming
antichrist will rise from east like phoenix,
radiant wings cloak canopy

whole world wide catastrophe, global ministries
bulk mail this story
to our big box in the country,
leave out part about economy and possibility

i was always terrified of being left behind,
when rapture comes, folks airlifted, disappeared
me left at the kitchen counter with the hum of refrigerator
and a jar of american peanut butter

here i am, mister president,
here i am pop, still alive
with my head and my feet
and my mind

my little house in the country
was in the united states of america
under dad nixon dad johnson
dad reagan and bush

smaller pops in the usa say,
if i was in his shoes
i'd do the exact same thing
to protect my family

my country tis of thee, sweet land of fibbery
let freedom ping, red poppies of blood
on green field tapestries, speckled mussolini,
hitler, franco, bush

i am, from the country, one country,
one land, indivisible, by dad
who said *everywhere*
was some pop's pad?

pirates den ritual

pirates den bar on kettner boulevard, by airport
san diego 2005

i used to be apple tree, but i am home here now
suddenly, i grow palm tree tall, san diego's getting small

standing at kettner, in a chain link lot
flight path, rocks the world

molars grind in passenger mouths, cocooned in 747s
will terrorists body snatch, hustle us in zippered bags to afterlife?

is osama bin laden, the antichrist? is george bush possessed?
inside marine layer night, i shake out my palm fronds and breathe in eucalyptus

bass beats cascade from pirates den and baptize parking lot
i stand sanctified, in lemonade darkness,

california? queenie? please open the gates for me, i invoke,
mister subterranean root doctor,

i beseech thee, anoint the roots that heat the soles of our feet,
on mamas in bagdad, kids playing soccer in afghanistan

mister down low dirt worker, earthquake rearranger, *we are far
from the best we can dream*

mister exorcist specialist of the whole capitalist order of missighted dads
if you got a bulldozer, we could sure use a hand

borders

i live in a city with edges
to the east desert fire, to the west dunes, salt water
to the north, border check, to the south, barbed wire

a border is a metaphor for a story of two countries
not what land had in mind, not in body's rhyme
foot knows to love thigh hip, heart knows body breath lip

a country is a metaphor for a story of "what's mine"
but countries are just arbitrary lines
not what land has in mind,
not in stars' design, not in mountain's rhyme

countries are just arbitrary lines,
ignored by hurricane, twister, breath
breathe in, hold, blow up, red

countries are not in, body's breath
breathless, coroner separates flesh
officials dress what's left, in flag

honeysuckle mint, miss presidential address
foot knows to love thigh hip,
face knows lilacs,
the smell of peppermint

east-west

I.

i lived in morocco in 1990
there were no evening helicopter checks for scared kids in hoods
and no freeways to drive as free individuals, one car at a free time

i went to a wedding in the high atlas mountains, and when the road ended
i met a boy tending sheep
we sat together, in crickets and silence

it gets lonesome, coming up in the country,
i remember pulling tansy ragwort, weeds the cows couldn't eat,
and being ecstatic to meet, soldiers in war paint,
trudging through swamp, looking for Fort Lewis, totally lost
i wonder if this shepherd kid, met some of them, too,
i wonder what, they chose to do

the shepherd and i talked with our faces, because we didn't share much language
he touched index finger to lip before he greeted me, and when i made to go
he placed his palm against his heart, reached in pocket, and gave me a favorite rock
said "i mean it" with his hand and eyes, like we learn to pledge allegiance
but there were no flags between us
just some sheep and crickets, a young boy's brown eyes

II.

when u.s. news finally aired the gulf war
reporters stated areas size of "football fields"
were wiped out with each sure-shot-scud missile
but we weren't in the super bowl,
and when bombs hit, there were faces in it
fragile stuff, kids, trying to just grow up,

47

in places where folks still work earth to live
in places where they'd never heard
of astro-turf
i went south toward sahara
where the revolutionary blue touregs live
their foreheads and necks glow indigo
when sweat wets dye from long swathes
of head wraps

on the way, saw a trucker pulled off,
kneeling at dusk, saying prayers
sky was tangerine, hills cast grays and greens
god was everywhere

III.

in sahara, the dunes lean back and rest,
like a worker man lies pecs-up,
after a long day of labor
blue metallic lizards skitter, across their sand chest
and tall ornery camels with big yellow teeth
and little kids coaxing them, give rides to foreigners, for a few dirhams
some of these kids wear yankee baseball caps,

warm goat skin drums by fire
make music and dance with each other, when the day's work is done
at night in the heat, folks climb on roof to sleep
with wind and stars and moon

IV.

dear lord, subterranean doctor, anoint the roots that heat
the soles of our feet, for mamas in bagdad,
kids playing soccer in afghanistan,

48

californians clinching sand
hear our ceptors back-talk,
from wiry evergreens, wind shot
electric orange madrones
and spindly palms, topheavy in thought,
speak in green dread-locks

atlantic and pacific are not so far apart, draw us moon
to breath between us, eucalyptus peppermint
the best we can dream it, skating on the edge
of lemons and concrete

V.
Red

come-inside-red

red purrs round orb   full   satisfied
like sitting in shade by late summer roses   in their loose lips   my face, just fits

red purrs round orb   full   satisfied
like breathing in cedar sauna air   pleasure cat curl purr

red purrs round orb   full
on my girlfriend's   saturday-night-skirt-hips   satisfied

red   shines on mama's lips, droops in bows on black braids
dragon tall   in chinatown on new year's day

red   snug in paper sheath   boxed in click crayola case
red waits
afraid   between a twelve year old's legs
sticky   in a rhododendron throat

hummingbird red   buzz purr girl
round belly bloom juice satisfied

rose faces floaton still waters deep red kid
monkey-arm-hanging from sapling   bouncing   blind into snare

nobody told you   there was nothing you could do
little-girl-red   better-run-red   better-off-dead   red

rockabye baby girl woman child   all-better-now-red
caterpillar   cocoon

red sky at night   this storm shall pass

rage

my rage is in my feet, because they couldn't run fast enough
my rage is in my belly, because it felt it

a punch in the stomach,
got sick, wasn't tough enough to take it

my rage is in my forehead,
tangled red

my rage is on these butter keys, on the screen,
in my crunchy knees

my rage is in the air,
in the atmosphere

in trampled wood slats, under the tap dancer's
tap tap tap, snap

my rage is beside me, blinking
pleading for me to give it breath

rage, i spit you like a river death
i lay you to rest

butterfly

my edges are, filaments of moth wing
tissue paper, between finger tips

caterpillar lithe, green girl
no mouth or limbs to fight

alight, on fence
in wing, delicate as hymen

pulsing, black red
hush now, rest

these are, the butterfly times
breathing in, growing whole, breathing out, letting go

54

yellow plastic princess

yellow plastic princess   prance girl   ride
slip-n-slide
run splat   five year old thighs
up jump skip it
hip switch queen/ie

i'm just five
i have a white bikini with polkadots and a ruffle on my behind
i play sexy, like i'm my aunties, put socks in my top, and pull my bottoms down
i pretend naked, magic, secret
i'm not afraid of anything
dare me

I.

i was the kind born sexy-headed
there are these kinds of children
who daydream
nasty   innocent

some men don't understand this or care
they enter to steal what's precious rare
and few women step to protect their chicks
like the Hen story tells it

instead they try tricks, swaddling in tights
overcoat shields, against eye fire licks
waiting to eat you like kindling and spit you to ashes

grown-ups say, *you asked for it, switching like that*
you don't act right, in some outfits

55

II.

that's how i lost my swimsuit
and how the trouble came
secret, naked
ashamed
happy go lucky got heavy with buckets of blame
semi-truck loads of top soiled pain

worse, she cracked
her spirit went awol to find a safe place
to the popcorn glitter then outer space
holy ghost broke in with *nobody home*
ransacked everything,   down to bare bones

plastered
she used her head to paste seams between
pretty jezebel   virgin daughter
her spirit clean split
no way it could fit

call me zombie, shuffling in a house of skin
down here i hear kin, hollowed out, mounted,
bucking to make it

III.

norene

haunted by her dead dad, spittin' mad, but he's not alive to kill
she sticks pins in dolls and prays for him to stop his calls

invokes banshees, warlocks, u.s. torture techs
to scour what she can not forget

she sat bed-side for six months as he withered
no other family would visit tyrant, alcoholic, belligerent but daughter dutiful deliberate
signed papers, waited, walked to na meeting onion peeling counseling on night
after night enterings into alice-n-wonderland sheets
now it's inheritance and splitting up remnants
she says, *i had to have sex with him, and what do i get?*

mama chose blindness, hard to keep your girl in plain sight
when you're married to a pedophile   papa

IV.

melody

worries she's too light to walk
see through glass girl, paper breeze
dissolve, spring snow

maybe his memory is stored in fat cells
body logic, reason, what's your story?
treason, rather starve than remember that time of living

but body's duty is to survive
pump blood breath cuss, live regardless
buck up body, march on

i remember how cute she was coming up husky
not string bean like her sister

maybe being more lean would have saved her
don't know why he fancied her,

teacher in lutheran school

V.

all the little children you love so shepherdly
diamond, saffron treasure child
without fortune

where is your precious love?
where is your saving grace?

i've been quiet, listening, ears stretched to catch that bleating beacon, lamb of light
but i'm afraid to walk on water

you can't walk because your load's too heavy
you have some shit to drop, other stuff to carry,   *so girl, what you got?*

magic nasty secrets, dare-mes, yellow plastic, polka dots
i guess there's quite a lot

you'll make it

up jump skip it, water hopper
prance that carpet, slip-n-slide
hip   switch   queen

strip show

vista point, national, truck tires roll, rest
monument woman flesh, my friend's the best
"woman power" you say me sideways,
shoulders back, dancehall wall, the niñas
de tus ojos smile, Tecate tilt, swallow

she is Moses   and the sea
stone men molten, wave golden,
orbs roped, tetherball pole, drain-suck-pull,
palm slap, melt down, round
rubber rims, slot canyon lips,
heels grind, ground swells,
feet, balls, flex
eyelids cheshire, stretch

she vacates, dreams hot Beaumont rain love
blue is the mountain, as the sunshine in my heart
string bean, freckle head, brown baby spins
toes squish smooch, red dust muds
heels click wood slats, she comes back,
like a double head screwgun,
two worlds, in one

full face smile open neck stretch
collar bone ridge road, moonlight ice, fresh sweat bright,
up-cup breasts bubble tip bop, dance, try to walk
torso ramps,
half bowls, tight
hips figure eight, radiate
butta butta butt whips, copter blades

tablas beat, texas storm heat, thighs burst skirt
lips wink, thong strip licks, ass laughs
toes talk fast, through sandal-strap cracks

i am, in dip between index and middle, of her fisted hand
grip hips steady fire man
tongue lip lime pulp, tequila salt coarse kiss
you don't let go my hand,
breath skin she we land sea,
look lava in my eyes, say me,
"woman power, comes from inside"

Blessing

exorcise me, lay hands on and weep holy ghost rain
wash me in river talk, head cocked
use your gift of tongues
swaddle me in amazing graces
brush my cheeks in rose of sharon eyelashes
whisper, sweet jesus name kisses

anoint my feet
like jesus did for mary magdalen
embrace me, like the prodigal son
let me come home to you, broken and blue
rock me, in the bosom of abraham
open your chest man
and let god do the rest

june gloom

I.

june gloom is san diego in most gorgeous gray
greens and golds exhale stretch

in cool lapping light, gray calms, welcomes
salt air in sinuses

shadow spots
sitting under awnings, green leaves, sky tops

gray's the good gloom that stops
gray sighs, recognizes it is still alive

II.

gloom blooms red poppies on italian hillside
red guelaguetza, skirts flip

drummers thunder, palm pink pads
red, gloom, good

III.

i said i'd take it, if the choice is gloom and god
red and white, shadow and light

i said i'd take it all,
if this is what i'm dealt, in this life

i'll take the boredom, and the strife,
i'll take the knife, i'll take the kiss

i'll take seared steak and mushrooms
and livingroom dances, on carpet and linoleum

i'll take hand in hand walks
at twilight on sand, in santo tomas

i'll take your hand cupping my head
i'll take the 'beautiful' you give me, the laughter you pull from me

i'll take this all, and patty cake the many into one
patchwork prince story

gloom? that there has been no perpetual bloom, no golden anniversary
my generation, of women, must make our own, holidays

Sliver

you're working your way out of me
and it hurts, still, too many and too big
to let dad dig you out

and he can't pin me, i'm too big
besides, my elements are more than earth
and that pocket knife won't work

shovel maybe, but that would really hurt
i am more than dirt, opalescent
violet air, teal red, vapors

sugar, you don't melt
walk through this rain
you can stand the pain

take a hot bath
plunge in lake, go down deep
dead-man-float, soak

he'll raise up, in bits of stick
skin reddens, splits, he gunks out
assembles, in stories of twig

then he will be there, and you will be you
from one, back to two—have faith, this is true
they work themselves out, slivers, they do

VI.
BLACKBERRIES

whatever helps her struggle

her body is beautiful, from the side, she's an *s*
and she's generous, when she greets friends she gifts

a full hug, a soft hug, a one-and-only hug, a special body hug,
with her breasts and arms and smells and laughter

she's not the type to think about her looks much, she's an intellectual
her husband too, still, they love to flirt, with everyone

they watch, with eyes like lit match
together they spark, from heads

to hands to ass to lips, impish, tricksters
time to use your magic tricks

rock steady babies, batten down, *be shelter through this storm*

lately, his mind's a hornets' den
rearranging, planning, negotiating fate

i promise to do my best to get her pregnant as she wishes,
i promise to argue less over dishes, hold hands more

make more dinners, put down newspaper and books, look up
watch when she dances, appreciate her, fate

i will do anything, even,
have a pesky kid, if you let her live

in this case, sperm is an offering, gold on a plate
just take it, let's shake, there's no time to waste

rock steady baby, keep them safe, fate, give them *shelter through this storm*

she called my friend and i to her—here, feel it, i want you to know
what it's like, press hard, go ahead, i have no inhibition

i can't tell you how many doctors have probed me these past days
and feel around to my armpit, this is where *it hopped*

and why i have to start chemo, quickly, wait—i can't find it!
he stood up and rushed to her standing on carpet with shirt held up

pressed his small hands under armpit, on side of right breast
pulsed fingers—found it, here!

we came in to touch—feel it? we nodded
it was solid, truth

at dinner she announced, we're going to have a baby, he's finally relented,
winking across table at him, smiling at us on either side, but it's not funny to him

breast cancer is less common in women,
who have been pregnant, she explained

if hope was a gaze, he made it, for her, not descendants
eyes set on her face, rigid as cable, *whatever helps her struggle*, he said

that night, they kept dropping what they were doing to embrace
curling into each other's nooks, caress is different than before, everything's changed

rock steady baby, keep me safe, *be my shelter through this storm*

69

flame

i miss her when she wore red lipstick
when she was vivacious
when her grasp was firm
when she gripped you with her gaze
and shook you

i miss her when she wore flame
taffeta, to our parties in north park
when she danced like cindy lauper and didn't worry
about academic papers or hard lumps
of cancer

i miss her when her eyes talked tricks
from deathbed in climate controlled clinic
when she demanded green frosting cake and candles
for her husband's birthday and for what she named
her *pre-funeral party*

i miss her when we all had plenty of time
before the vultures got in line
to do their duty, tough guts
they can eat it, chemo
morphine, goldenseal
gallons of green tea,
baby you fought hard, tried

my bald winged
pallbearers,
carry her please
to the otherside

Stretched

I step off the plane at Sea-tac, sniff like a rottweiler, big face, shaking head,
slobber ring, round moon beam, making sense, of things

wet air, river rock, moss, drenched dirt, swamp fog
I smell it, tumbles down the sky bridge, waves cool

Up through the concrete parking garage
Washington Yelm Tacoma, Nisqually Delta, Mount Tahoma

Airport asphalt and corporate development can't, cover you up
I am home

And already bruised with the ache of losing you
too many times of tying up, tying down, umbilicus rewound

On departure I am a taut trapeze
and I am gone, too long, these days

Mama's 'hi honey' clips the cord
and I collapse like a metal slinky

This steady yearning makes me only un-spooled thread,
a yodel from the Bald Hills, dark green smells

Phoebe Rae

Phoebe Rae, you came out slippery
dark hair swirls, one chubby shoulder
then another, little ornery face

Bright light and cut safety line, lower lip quivering
loud! sucking fist fast, found tiny thumb,
Nurse said, *clever kid*

Born September 24th 2003 at eight forty five pm
Libra, on the tail end of the moon,
sliver thin streak, gleaming
like a miner's dream
in black night

And it was still warm
we were rainless, no snow fell on even the highest places
and the days/ came/ dry

Summer stayed for dessert,
breathing trees Fire Engine Red cake
turning leaves and hazing sun, vanilla ice cream

On the horizon, Mount Rainier bared her rock body bold,
got real with old friend red Mars, he came back round
chuckled after with giddy stars

Down low, kids ran across the country with sparklers in sweaty fists
on plywood sheets, spun flowers hissed, fuchsia gold
and firecrackers flipped, sound wave wakes

This was the time when you came, Phoebe Rae,
ocean rolled through your mama, she pushed with all her might
passed you through the Ring of Fire
and gave you to the Light

blackberry pie

is kernels of juice
blue, mom makes it do
magic heat to vanilla ice cream
purple dream

there were many nice things,
the corduroy pinafore
the daily notes in lunch sack
of a smiley face and curly cue hair
your mama loves you, and *do great*
with a thermos of homemade soup

dad too, he rocked me on front porch
after seven yellow jacket stings
i howled through the valley
in baking soda paste
while he sang, *in the big rock candy mountain* . . .

but just like grandma vernon always said
don't bother doing anything nice for your children
they'll only remember the bad things, anyway
like when she tethered my dad
to the front yard tree
so he could play when she was at work

was that bad? a ruined childhood?
bless her heart
and pie too, is sometimes
tart

About the Author

Jenifer Vernon was raised in Yelm, Washington. As a young girl she wrote down the stories of her elders in the local vernacular, sparse and direct speech. She says, "I learned that plain old words can shine glorious if they are bowed and rearranged right—and that sometimes the rhythm says more than the words themselves." Later she journeyed abroad, to Spain and Morocco, working on oral history projects in conjunction with her studies at Evergreen State College. She earned an M.A. in International Studies at the University of Oregon and a Ph.D. in Communication at the University of California, San Diego. She has been a featured poet in clubs and performance spaces in the San Diego-Tijuana area and has presented papers on performance poetry and its role in community building at a number of venues. *Rock Candy* is her first book-length publication.

Author's Note

Many of these poems are inspired by the lives of actual people and events. However, when the facts have not been available in their entirety, the author has imagined some of the story. The poem "Elegy for Chastity" was propelled by the murder of the author's childhood friend, Chastity Bartram (1970-1998) and importantly, other women like her. It aims to give voice to a collective and an individual through poetic eulogy. Some of the family narratives speak across the poems as related characters give their points of view and symbols from the stories reappear in new settings. Finally, commas, word divisions, and words dropped out of a sentence often follow the spoken rhythm crafted for the line.